The Magical
Wisdom of Kids

Deborah Masters

"The Magical Wisdom of Kids" is printed on
sugar cane paper to respect the kids' request to
protect trees. They also asked us to respect the
earth, so the paper used is acid-free,
biodegradable and recyclable.

Global Truth Publishing
Sausalito, California

Table of Contents

The Magical Wisdom of Kids

Global Truth Publishing
1001 Bridgeway, Suite 474
Sausalito, CA 94965 USA
415.331.1102
www.globaltruthpublishing.com
sales@globaltruthpublishing.com

ISBN.0-9740465-1-5
Library of Congress Control Number:
2004116467

Cover, graphic design, and illustrations
by Claudia Uscátegui

Wholesale discounts are available to
resellers and special discounts are
available on bulk purchases of this book
for educational and fundraising purposes
and for use as premiums, incentives, and
promotions. For details, please contact
the publisher.

Acknowledgments

This book is dedicated to children everywhere—may you

inherit a world worthy of your wisdom.

It is with deep affection and gratitude that I thank the many

people, friends and family who gave of their hearts, talents

and resources to help with the creation of this book. May your

lives be filled with joy and laughter, and may you always keep

the magical spirit of a child alive within you.

A special heartfelt thanks to the kids who graciously

consented to be interviewed for this book.

It should be noted here that they preferred to be called "kids"

rather than children.

People often ask me how I found the children quoted in this book, and how I was able to get them to speak so openly and profoundly from their hearts and minds. My response is that I did not find them, their wisdom found me. And, because children still glow with the light from whence we all come, they speak easily with a clear remembrance of important and sacred things. Very little was required of me—except to ask, and then to listen.

The kids did not know in advance what I was going to ask them. It was a privilege to experience the simplicity, depth, feeling, and sincerity with which these kids spontaneously answered the questions. They spoke with an authority that was compelling and a directness that was clear, simple, and at times humorous. Their words made me laugh and cry. I was often rendered speechless as I took in the magnitude of their wisdom. I became a student in the presence of a sage. I stepped out of time and into timelessness, greeted by the knowledge I once knew, and was able to remember again through the grace of these children.

During the course of the interviews, four distinct themes emerged: Love, God, Peace, and Healing. The book has therefore been divided into those four sections. The visions and ideals of the first three sections come together in the fourth chapter, "Healing for a Better World". Here the kids put their values to work—they offer specific prescriptions for bringing the world into harmony.

With rare exception, the kids' language has not been editorially "improved." These are their natural, uncensored voices. Some have been translated into English from another language. The informal style of capitalization, punctuation, and other grammatical conventions reflects the kids' own informal speaking styles and rhythms. Not everything that each child said could be included, but whether a child contributed one line or many, each contribution, like each child, is unique and precious.

Read slowly and carefully; enjoy their every word. Their purity deserves to be honored, their humor enjoyed, their innocence revered. These kids will inherit the Earth, and in these pages they ask us to leave them a world of peace, beauty, and prosperity. They also tell us how. Their magical words are calling us back to that spontaneous wise heart and mind that lives in all of us. Listen deeply.

Deborah Masters, January 2005

Introduction

Love
sweet and pure

like a bird flying

to its freedom

love longs to wrap

its golden arms around you

two heads resting together

Love

like a stream clasping

to its bed of moss

and a summer day

lingering in the sky

a child runs into a mother's soft caress

and love opens its eyes even wider to the world

Zoe Loughran Brezsny, 12

Through the eyes of Love

Love is a feeling that you should give away.
Albert Brown, 8

L O

The light inside everyone is called love.
Liesel Staubitz, 6

It's important to love people because we all have families. We should all take care of babies. We should all love each other, and...

it's not okay if you don't brush your teeth.

Isabel Rauchle, 3

V E

Love is happiness

Steven Chen, 9

Love is compassion.

Spencer Palmer, 10

Being with children is *love*.

Children are filled with light from the heavens.

Being with a child is feeling *love* all around.

Love feels like a radiation, or a golden fluid,

like when it's raining;

it's like golden drops filling your body.

Love is a simple thing;

it's a pure warmth that fills our body.

Zoe Loughran Brezsny, 12

Love is peace. *Benny Bakar, 8*

Love
is respecting yourself
and other people.

Elyssa Armstrong, 9

I am nice to the people I love, and I try to
make them feel good about something they
didn't do good at.

Lauren Steinbaum, 12

If you love someone, you take care of them. And
if someone loves you, they take care of you. When
someone loves me, I feel it in my tummy.
I feel married.

Nicole Childers, 5

I can tell I love someone when
I take care of them and when
I hold them…and…I can just tell. I can
feel love in my heart. It's kind of calm and I
feel really
really good.

Leah Grillo, 8

really good, but a good kind of weird.

Alon Sacks, 5

Love people for who they are,
and not for who they aren't.

Sophie Gilchrist, 11

I feel love in my heart; it feels weird, but a good kind of weird.

When you love
someone,
your heart brights up.

Mallory Bragg, 8

Love makes me feel good, and safe.

Matthew Schabel, 7

12

Love is when you care for someone and if they're hurt you help them.

Aaron Smith, 9

Love is when you like someone
so much more than anything.
It is greater than
great. If you love someone
so much sometimes you kiss them
and hug them. If you are a grown-up
you could marry them.
Love makes you feel so good in
your heart.

Madison Naomi Schobinger, 6

Love means peace,
understanding,
and caring.

Anji Herman, 10

Love is light.
Love makes me feel happy.
Love is a toy store.

Theo Chamberlain, 3

Everyone has love.

Look inside.

Everybody has it.

It's a feeling.

Use love every day to help the world out.

Sarah Wiener, 13

Love is something very special. You can see love anywhere, really, if you look for it, like a rose opening.

Elsinore Smidth, 13

Love is something inside. It's a strong feeling that makes you show kindness to people and nature.

Elena Scott, 12

Spreading peace in the world is love.

Haley Pacheco, 11

Love is Happy!

Jacqueline Norton, 3

Love is caring and sharing and giving everything
that matters to other people. You can love a lot of
people in different ways, but it is all love if you care
and share. When you love, it is fun every day and
when you are loved, you feel protected and important.

Lauren Moscarello, 8

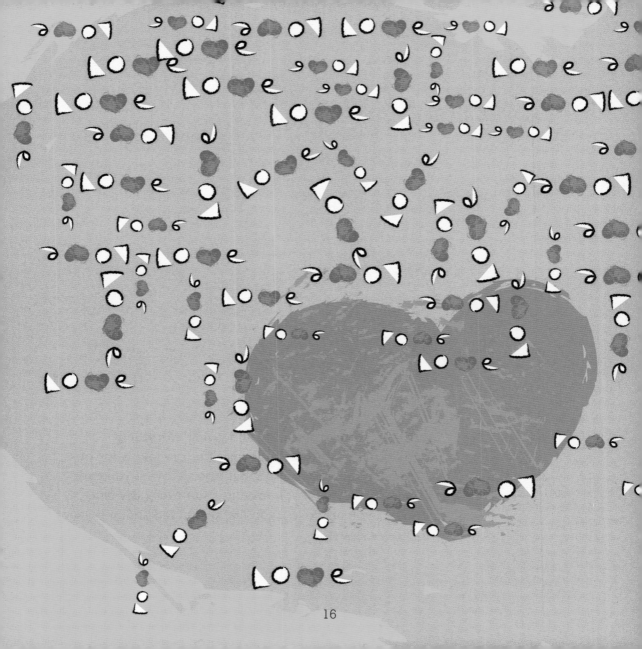

16

Love is when someone has a passion for someone else, when they feel happy together.

Jill Meserve, 11

I feel love in my tummy.

Zoe Goldberg, 6

Love is a tingly feeling that's hard to explain. When you're deeply thinking about someone you love, you can't help but smile deeply. You should behave in the kindest manner possible towards the ones you love.

Lilah Clevey, 11

Love is something that we think, we feel, we do. People who love you give you hugs and support you every day and they look out for you. That's how you know they love you—they help you through hard times and they urge you on when you think you're doing something you can't do. They're just always there for you.

TJ Dempsey, 11

Love is how you feel about someone else. It makes you happy. I know someone loves me when they want to spend time with me. They drop everything if I need their help and they do whatever it takes to make me feel better or give me what I need if it's important.

Coray Runge, 13

Love would be when you really really care for someone and you do a lot for them and you wouldn't forget about them and you care for them almost more than you would care for yourself.

Cortnay Cymrot, 10

It's good to hug people. It's important to tell people *"I love you."* I love you as much as the sky stays!

Anya Rauchle, 6

I feel love in my whole body, in my heart...I don't feel my heart booming when it happens, it's just kind of throughout me.

Chelsea Cymrot, 12

Love is caringness, to be helpful, to show kindness to other people.

Ari Bental, 9

Love is respecting and being kind to others. I love you to the stars and back!

Alex Rauchle, 7

Love is your best friend and family and even your special blanket.

Catherine Raissipour, 9

18

When someone from my family says *"I love you,"* it makes me feel good and makes me feel that someone is there for me. Other love, between boys and girls not in the same family, is different. That love is kind of tickly—a little more embarrassing. It's way different.

Elliott Stone, 12

I love animals; if you love them they love you. It's good to have animals because if you had a bad day you could just go cuddle up with them and tell them all that's happening, and you'll feel like somebody's really listening.

Carrie Brandon, 9

Love is when you like someone a lot, and you play with them and talk with them. Love feels good. I love my dog and cat and I feed them and pet them. We should love animals.

Lucia Simon, 6

Love is not only hugging or kissing your mother. You have to have respect for love to be real.

Alisa Billig, 9

I love my cat Midnight, except she's a bit pouncey—she pounces everywhere.

Lilly Barnett, 7

I don't know much about love, but I love my friend Forrest. I hug him.

Cole McCann-Phillips, 3

…they always have time to listen to something
I have to say.

Leah Grillo, 8

…Mom sings me to sleep and she does hand massage.

Tyler Briant Nierstedt, 6

…Daddy kisses and hugs me and tells me he loves me
when he wakes me up.

Madison Naomi Schobinger, 6

…they hug me and tuck me in at night, and cheer
me up when I'm sad. My mom teaches me new
recipes that she learned from her mom. Love feels
great.

Kaylie Kathleen Williams, 10

...they hug and kiss
me and protect me.

Tyler Mahoney, 4

...my mama gets things down for me that I can't reach. She looks for things that I lost. I like to make pictures for my mom and tell her she can take them to work, so they remind her of me. Love is like when you make a heart, it kind of reminds me of love. People should make a card that says **I Love You.**

Katherine Mary Scotnicki, 5

...they help me with homework and take me on vacations because they want me to see other places.

Lauren Christianson, 10

...my mom gives me breakfast: my favorite is when she makes me strudel with icing.

Matthew Schabel, 7

Mommy loves me 'cause she likes
   me and wants me to get healthy
   and strong. Daddy loves me, he
   likes me and he's happy, 'cause his
   grandparents and his mom love
   each other and loved him
   when he was a little boy and a big
   boy and when he was a teenager.
   Animals love me but they don't
   hurt me; they like me 'cause I'm
   nice to them, 'cause they love me
   back—they give me kisses, they
   lick me. Even Stormy licks me.
   [Stormy is a horse]

Malia Kristina Bertelsen, 4

Love is quiet.
If people get sick
in the belly,
I help them.

Taylor Childers, 5

Love is joy and happiness and good
feelings about someone. If someone's
nice to you, if they're kind and help
you, then you know they love you.

Karl Bach, 11

Love is a good feeling: it's having
someone you can talk to, and that
you know loves you.

Evan Steinbaum, 12

I feel love when I'm at home doing
things with my family.

Lauren Christianson, 10

I feel love in my
heart. It is a warm
feeling inside.

Molly McCann, 10

If I think about
who I love,
I feel something inside.
There's a feeling that
tells me, like someone is
inside me, sort of like the
real me is inside me,
keeping track of
everything, reminding me
of what everything is.

Cole Page, 12

If I love someone...

...I take care of them—so if someone
  got hurt, I would get them an ice pack.

Liesel Staubitz, 6

...it means they are in my heart and
  they keep me safe and that they love
  me back, I hope.

Elena Crowe, 8

...it means I am not alone.

Moki Kawaguchi, 8

...I'm glad they're around.

Vikas Arun, 9

...it means they are my friend and
  they trust me.

Schuyler Yedlin, 8

...I help them. I'm trying to heal
  Grandma. She needs it. It's very hard
  for her to do things. I touch her and I
  try healing her. She says it's making
  her feel better.

Joshua Slaughter, 8

...I'll do good favors for them and
  be nice to them, most of the time.

Max Goodley, 8

...and they were sick, I'd write them a
  note and send them a present to
  make them feel better. If one of my
  friends were getting picked on, I
  would stand up for them.

Jacob Dorfman, 8

...I care about them and help them
  and think about them all the time.

Sneha Krishnan, 9

Love is

strength, *hope,*
the heart,
the value of life,
the ability,
the innocence.

Juan Bernardo Uscátegui, 4

Love is when you look in someone's eyes and they really smile.

Robert Lehmann, 9

Love is when you like someone
a lot, a lot, a lot!
Good night, Mommy, I love you.
I love you all the way down to
the bottom of the ocean and then back up!
I love you all the way to
heaven and back
and that's a long way!

Zane Schobinger, 4

Love is when two people are nice to each other. Love is also like in nature—like I love animals. And when you love things, you take care of them.

Cali Slepin, 8

When somebody borns you it means they love you because it is your baby.

Lucy Black, 6

I feel love under a rainbow. I've seen a real rainbow before. I remember two of the colors, red and orange.

Tyler Mahoney, 4

When I love someone
I want to hug them.
I want to marry them.
I love princesses.
I love elephants.
I love my light,
and I love you.

Sophia Scorcia, 4

Loving is caring
for people and
things—a dog,
or a bird.
Happiness is to do
things for other
people; when
you do, it makes
you feel good
and it makes
them feel good.

Emma Rubinowitz, 11

I love animals.
I like their
sounds—how
they run.
The animals are
special to me.
When animals
get shot,
I get really sad.

Mallory Bragg, 8

LOVE means
God makes you
hug each other.

Gabriel Newbrum-Mintz, 2

31

Unknown, unseen, felt
you come from above
where stars always shine
light surrounds you inside and out

you give the fruit of your soul

to the people
and

embroider a sorrowful heart

a smile is life giving

your hands soothe a
worried face

like a ripple in a stream

you flow in and out of life

Siena Hood, 12

God has many faces

I think of God as an **angel** or a **sparkly beautiful flower.**

Emmy Wagner, 12

G

is a word of **hope.**

Angelique Traub, 12

God is **quiet**

Andy Chan, 3

34

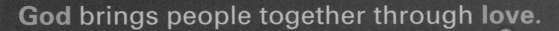

God brings people together through **love.**

Zeena Ojjeh, 9

God is not necessarily a **"he"** or **"she"**; it's the **universe**, the **atmosphere**. If God were a picture, God would be a **scene of nature** showing the broad heavens and stars.

Zoe Loughran Brezsny, 12

35

I do believe that
whatever God is,
it is good,
so maybe
God is LOVE

Lauren Moscarello, 8

I think there's not
really one God but
it's really like the
God in you.

Siena Hood, 12

God made everyone alive,
so we should treat each other nice.
God lives in the sky really far away.
We can't see him.
God lives inside us too.

Caleb Mahoney, 6

God is everything that is beautiful.
If you see a pretty flower, it's God.
If you see a homeless man
that has a twinkle in his eye, that's God.
Anything or anyone that is special to you
is in some way God.

Julia Egger, 13

God is a spirit that keeps you living. God is many things; he could be your hair. God is in the Arctic Ocean. God is everything.

Eleanor Silverstein, 9

God lives in heaven and with us.

Kylee Larsen, 12

God is air.

Lucia Simon, 6

God is a friendly spirit. It feels that God is alive, and I know that God is made of love. Sometimes I make wishes to God for a nice friend.

Mallory Bragg, 8

I think God lives in the heavens, somewhere in
   outer space. Sometimes I dream of going to heaven
   and there's this big arch and that's God's house.
   I don't really know what happens in heaven since I
   haven't been there; but I imagine that it's a place with
   flowers and you can do anything you want, like fly.

Alexandra Goldstein, 10

God is the Creator that created everything: trees, people, knowledge.
God gives you hands, arms, a body, and a mind so you can live.
God lives on the other side, in the spirit world.

Thomas Medicinehorse, 12

I like the idea there is God and that everything that
   happens is supposed to happen and that you can't stop
   something from happening. I do believe you can
   change your destiny. You are still going to go in one
   direction instead of another one, but you can
   bend it a little bit.

Ciro Podany, 12

God is looking over us, and his spirit is up in heaven.

Liesel Staubitz, 6

God is full of love and wants
to help us in every way possible,
but he lets us go through
different experiences so
we can **love,** get angry, and
show our emotions.
God is everywhere, in everyone.
God takes half of himself and
puts it in everyone so that they
have a **spirit** and can live and walk.
God's in every living thing:
plants, animals, people.

Justin Jones, 11

God is a person who was a king. He takes care of people up in heaven like Auntie Naomi and our dog Tessie. They are very happy in heaven because everyone is nice in heaven. There are a lot of angels in heaven. In a book that Daddy and I read, when an animal goes to heaven then the kid angels take care of them. Do you think one of them has Tessie?

God is someone in my heart. He makes sure people don't fight. People don't ever fight in heaven because it is magical. When you die you go up to heaven and you get wings. The ones you have now on your back will get bigger when you get there.

God was a healer when he was alive. He healed people. He touched them and they were good and one time they were cheeters—no not cheeters—I can't remember—it's like a cheetah—they were very sick and they had sores all over them. [*Madison was trying to remember the word "lepers" and was relating it to the animal "leopard," but in her mind she got it confused with the word "cheetah" and came up with the word "cheeters."*]. He was a healer and he can heal anyone. When you are very sick he can sometimes heal you. I think he puts power down here [*in your heart*] and makes you feel good.

Madison Naomi Schobinger, 6

I think God is really old and he has a lot of wrinkles and he's part of church. **I think about God.** I actually think that God did make the world. I know that God made people.

Katherine Mary Scotnicki, 5

God looks like a skier and a chipmunk.

Nicole Childers, 5

Coco, I love you. I hope you have a fun time with God up in heaven. I miss you. I will see you when I die too, but it will take a long time for me to die. Coco is one of God's creatures and God looks after all his creatures.

Gigi Staubitz, 4

God is the biggest angel in the world. He looks like he is our father, and he is. He is all around us. He is standing behind you, Mama. He is watching over us.

Victoria Berggren, 7

God is bigger than anything. He doesn't shoot green slime **out of his ears.**

Sophia Scorcia, 4

If I feel bad and I want to talk to someone, **I talk to God.** Sometimes God answers.

Roza Trilesskaya, 8

God is both a God and a Goddess.

Elyssa Armstrong, 9

God is the protector, the maker of nature and the whole world. God looks both like a he and a she. God can come as an animal or a person to help all of us.

Sneha Krishnau, 9

God—she's a person who lives in heaven and you can always trust her and look up to her because she'll always be there. I talk to God when there's something bad happening in my family and ask her to heal them up.

Jill Meserve, 11

God lives in heaven and gives people and animals life and creates peace on earth. God is neither a man or a female but a spirit who created all.

Steven Chen, 9

44

I think God is like this: when you go to
heaven, the boys go to the boy
God, and the girls go to the girl God,
and whatever kind of animals, say
my dog, when he dies, he goes to the
doggie God. When my bunny dies,
he goes to the bunny God, and when
my bird dies, he goes to the bird
God, and so on and so on. God makes
them into a new person and
they come back as a different person.

A girl God might look like all the girls in
the world. She might have different parts
of our bodies, like she might have
freckles like me and some other people
that have freckles and then curly hair
or straight hair. Maybe she likes to wear
different color blush or makeup.
Same with the boys.

God could be anything and protects
everybody. God could be my dog right
now; he can just shrink into my
dog and when he wants to go back up,
he can just go back up.

Danielle Schatzman, 8

God is a baby, and crawls.

Tyla Doolin, 4

God's not a person because the wind is God. The wind loves me 'cause that's his Creator above him, 'cause the Creator lets every person see him. About God, he likes you back because he's so nice, 'cause he lets you do every single thing to him. God loves you very much 'cause he lets you love him. Clouds could turn into different things and something comes from the sky, 'cause the wind makes it wavy so we could do stuff like put our umbrellas underneath our heads.

Malia Kristina Bertelsen, 4

God speaks to you and

God is always with you. You could pray to him if you feel lonely.

Molly McCann, 10

Each religion sees God differently, but it's all the same God.

Vikas Arun, 9

The Dalai Lama is a God.

Theo Chamberlain, 3

God is a very helpful spirit.
God is many spirits for many religions.

Alon Sacks, 9

ays **in a tree** that **is fire,**

"You better appear."

Gabriel Newbrum-Mintz, 2

God is the creator, the inventor, the organizer of the universe. I don't talk to God on a regular basis but when something is desperate, like when I broke my leg and was in pain, I asked him questions like: *"How should I get through this? What will happen? Am I going to be okay?"* I didn't get an answer back but I'm okay now so I guess I did.

Coray Runge, 13

I don't think there's some big God that rules everybody and tells them what to do. Everyone has inside of them their own spirit that makes them grow.

Elsinore Smidth, 13

God will do things for you and he doesn't need your thanks, but it's polite to thank him.

Sophie Gilchrist, 11

47

God might be a cloud. *Anya Rauchle, 6*

Angels are a kind of bird, an angel bird, and they fly. *Abbie Benford, 5*

God is everything alive. He is not one person, one animal,

God is someone who creates things and people too. He make

God is Mother Earth so we should take care of her. *Lucy Black, 6*

God makes the world a good place for humans. *Arjay Jimenez, 9*

...he tree. He is within all of us, within our soul. *Ben Herrick, 11*

...erything grow and everything live. *Indigo George, 7*

God is a person that loves you a lot. *Gayle Henry, 12*

God is right here and right here,
to the left and right of me,
and under and above me. It's a boy,
even though I know it's not; it's always
referred to as a *"he,"* so it reinforces in my
mind that it's a boy. But I know it's not. But
they refer to him with a capital *"H."*
I don't think God is a person or a human.
He is everything. God is in the clouds and he
is looking down and he is on the ground
looking up and he is in this room and he can
be wherever you imagine him to be.

Chelsea Cymrot, 12

God hangs out in heaven and in our hearts.

Alexander Palmer, 5

God is in everything and God made everything
and everything is special the way that it is because it's
different. God is in plants and people and rocks.

Danny Sacks, 11

God is a cloud and he walks on them. God helps
people; he makes them walk and makes them move.
I talk to God in my bed. God makes me feel good.

Aaron Stone, 8

God is when you go on vacation.

Spencer Palmer, 10

God looks kind of
like Abraham Lincoln.
He has a beard.
You shouldn't tell
funny stuff about God.

Marcus Christianson, 6

51

I think **God** is me because
whenever I go to sleep
I feel him down in my **heart**.
It feels **kind** and **loving**.

Lilly Barnett, 7

God is love and spirit.
Spirit is light. Everyone has **light** in them.

Amanda Slaughter, 10

God takes care of people and keeps them company in heaven. People in heaven watch over us. Angels are like my grandma and grandpa; they stand on clouds and watch over their grandchildren because they love them. It makes me happy to know that my grandma and grandpa are watching over me.

Lucia Barnett, 7

I bring God into my heart through prayer. When you accept God into your heart you feel his love and grace. Sometimes you'll feel him pushing at your heart. Do what he tells you. Say he's trying to lead you somewhere, go there. Sometimes you'll have an experience and God uses that experience to shape you.

Timothy Josh Royal, 10

God is more of a thought, so I think
people just turn that thought into an
actual person, because it's easier
for people to believe in. I don't talk to
God but sometimes I feel like I'm
not alone, like walking down a hallway.

Angelique Traub, 12

The most important thing in life is
to love God with all your heart—even
if you don't, he loves you. It says
in the Bible that if you love God with
all your heart and all your soul,
he'll give you more love to give others.

Amy Elizabeth Royal, 12

God talks to me in my dreams. He says good stuff.
Sometimes he tells me what I'm going to do
the next day. **God** is a friend to us all, and nice,
and I hope he never leaves us.
God is good and handsome.

Joshua Slaughter, 8

I think that God is a power,

an energy source of some kind.

I really feel good about God, and

I know that God is cool.

God brings peace and

love to earth.

Connor Barnett, 8

God is the creator.

He is everywhere;

he is in every living thing.

He is good luck, good fortune.

Adrian Franco, 11

God doesn't have eyes or a mouth.

God is love. You can't call God a him or her;

it is simply love. There is no such thing as hell.

There is a personal hell

when you do something wrong;

you worry about doing things wrong.

Alisa Billig, 9

God is something that
created the earth and
helps things be right, and I think he's in every
space and I'd say he's in your heart,
because you love him—and that whatever he is,
he is really really great.

Ari Bental, 9

God helps us learn to
do a lot of hard things and helps us through
hard times.

TJ Dempsey, 11

God is a special kind of cloud
in the sky that helps dead people.
God is a man and a woman.
The man makes boys and the woman
makes girls. They have a house made
of clouds and eat rain. There is a hole
in the house which lets the sun shine in
to light up the house.
God has long long gray hair and a
beard and the woman God has long
curly hair down her back.
God has a toe ring and a
brown cat with a beard.

Samantha Collins, 7

I mostly think of God as sort of in the wind, but also in the clouds, and in heaven. God is a majestic grown man but not exactly—he's also transparent.

Terry Castleman, 9

God could be like a person, but also like everything else. If you saw a mouse, it could be God looking at you. God is really in everything.

Jacob Dorfman, 8

God belongs to the chapel and he loves little children.

Audrey Norton, 4

I think God is invisible.

He lives in the *wind* and in heaven.

He lives everywhere.

I think he has powers, but

I don't believe that he really

parted the Red Sea.

Marshall Levensohn, 9

God is **powerful**. God makes things grow and gives us food.

Elena Scott, 12

God is something that keeps me **safe** and **happy**.

Lila Hood, 8

God is *peaceful and loving.* He is good. God is in our hearts. I talk to God to tell him I'm sorry about something.

Afton Wight, 8

God means a *spirit* or the creator of Earth.

Matthew Schabel, 7

God is the *whole world, even you.*

Zoe Goldberg, 6

I think that God is more of a *spiritual force* that lives in everything; *it is everything.* I don't think God's a "he." I don't think it's any one thing. I think it can be whatever anyone wants it to be, many shapes and forms.

My dad's not that religious, but once his plane got hit by lightning, and he thought there was a bomb or something—he said a little prayer to God.

Eric Brandon, 13

I don't believe in God. The world just happened and no one knows how.

Alan Lefelman, 11

God is a perfect person who can do anything he wants. God is in heaven and everywhere and in everybody.

Jeremiah Byers, 12

60

God is what happens when nothing else can explain it.

Lilah Clevey, 11

Please remember the children of the dawning day
Do not let your anger dirty the waters of people's dreams
Give the world a future with no wrong way
Decide to dance a life that will say
Happiness and love a life that gleams
Please remember the children of the dawning day
Joy was never meant to fade away
Let your life smile a smile that beams
Give the world a future with no wrong way
Peace is a song that must play
With radiance and without one broken seam
Please remember the children of the dawning day
Give the world a future with no wrong way

Elsinore Smidth, 13

Give Peace a chance

Peace is when everyone is *getting along* in the whole world.

People need to respect everyone that lives.

Elliott Stone, 12

PEA

I think we need a bigger piece of peace.

Angelique Traub, 12

Peace would be when everyone is free.

Caleb Mahoney, 6

ICE

Peace can be as simple as a flower. It's not really one thing. It's an all around atmosphere.

Siena Hood, 12

peace

happy *friendship* *freedom*

...not like anything that's harmful; it's totally the opposite. You don't feel like you're in danger. And it's comfortable.

Molly McCann, 10

...freedom and the right to do what you want to do and stand up for your rights. People should have their heads straight and not be mean to other countries just because they have different rules than you.

Robert Lehmann, 9

...quiet and everyone likes each other. People don't hit each other or be mean to each other. They do not fight or hit someone with a real sword.

Madison Naomi Schobinger, 6

...the total opposite of war.

Aaron Smith, 9

...to treat people how you want to be treated.

Afton Wight, 8

...when you're cool and happy.

Kylle Koenig, 12

...friendship among people, or silence.

Kylee Larsen, 12

...no war; everybody is loving each other.

Spencer Palmer, 10

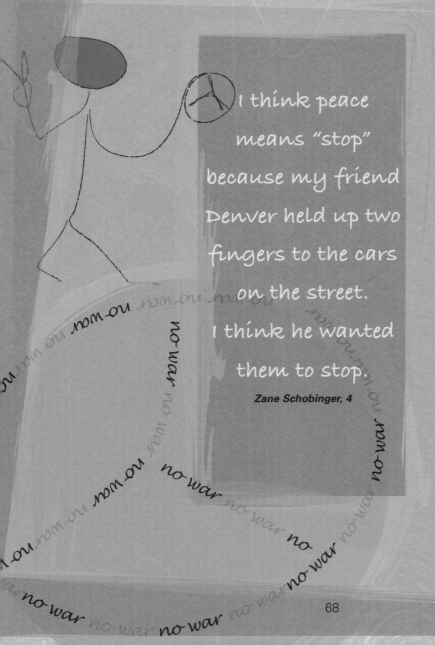

I think peace means "stop" because my friend Denver held up two fingers to the cars on the street. I think he wanted them to stop.

Zane Schobinger, 4

I think that war is stupid. Even if you try not to kill innocent people in a war, you probably would.

Lauren Steinbaum, 12

Peace is no fighting and no one getting angry for an entire day.

Alan Lefelman, 11

Peace is what everyone wants, where there is no fighting and trouble for anyone.

Steven Chen, 9

Peace is when there are no arguments between
people or nations.

Danny Sacks, 11

Peace means not harming anything and
being nice and trying to make friends, buying them
food or giving them a flower.

Alon Sacks, 9

Peace is calm. Listen to other people when
they're talking. Don't compete, because that makes
people fight.

Thomas Medicinehorse, 12

I don't think anyone likes war, except people who
are insane. I think a way of solving a problem is like
a tennis game or a soccer game.

Alex Leason, 12

War is like a
disease, and it
won't go away
until you take
the right
medication.

Marshall Levensohn, 9

Peace is more of a unity with everyone
being mostly equal. When I think of
peace, I think of everyone sharing
everything they have, and I think of
unlocked doors and everyone trusting
everyone. It's just like everyone
is united.

Cole Page, 12

If we lived in a peaceful world,
I'm not sure anyone would have made
up the game of football or hockey.

Justin Jones, 11

Peace makes you feel like you can
do anything you want. You can go buy
food. You don't have people who
say, *"go do this" and "go do that"*; it's
like freedom.

Aaron Stone, 8

When you're peaceful,
you are nice and friendly.

Nicole Childers, 5   Taylor Childers, 5

Don't fight with people because if
it starts in your family it will spread.
Start being peaceful first, and then
help the world.

Sarah Wiener, 13

Peace and understanding are the
important things to keep in mind.
War is a stupid idea. If people
have to settle something, they can
talk about it.

Anji Herman, 10

Peace is no fighting; it's just calm.
Fighting is not a good way to solve
problems. It's better to talk
things out.

Evan Steinbaum, 12

Peace is when you're quiet,
even with someone else.

Marcus Christianson, 6

Peace is when everyone likes
each other and they're being nice to
each other. There is no war, and
everything is calm and mellow. To not
have wars, the first thing I would
say is to get a president who doesn't
want to have wars. War isn't good
and peace would be a great thing. God
might be able to help, and love might
be able to help. Who knows?

Evan Cranston, 9

Peace is no fighting and no bossing people around.

Elyssa Armstrong, 9

Peace is joy, happiness with yourself, having mental peace, not stressed and feeling good. If the world were peaceful, there would be less world hunger and no discrimination. We would all be friends. There would be no reason to kill, no reason to hurt. You could just help. All the money and power that we put into our guns and bombs we could put into people who are in need.

Coray Runge, 13

Peace is no fighting. Kids in school are taught to not fight, to talk it over. Grown-ups are so far from school they don't really do that anymore. That leads to more wars and fights. It would be a better world if there was a lot more peace.

Alexandra Goldstein, 10

You should use your words instead of fighting; you should talk things out. If someone was being mean and made someone cry, I would tell them to say they are sorry. I don't give put-downs or make fun of someone.

Mallory Bragg, 8

Peace means that everybody is getting along and not giving each other a hard time (but if it's just teasing it's okay). And everybody kind of loving each other and caring for each other.

TJ Dempsey, 11

Life is a gift from God and he gave you the opportunity to live. You shouldn't waste it on war and killing. Don't kill each other. If there is a reason to kill, I haven't seen it. I hope that there will be all peace.

Ben Herrick, 11

Peace means No war you have a lot of joy.

Tyler Briant Nierstedt, 6

I wouldn't start a war.
Fighting is not love.
Be loving and kind.

Mattias Hanson, 10

Peace is when there is no war and hitting, no killing plants or animals.

Catherine Raissipour, 9

73

War is a combination of hatred and frustration. There should be a better way to resolve things. The things that I see on TV—bombs exploding—we shouldn't see these things, they shouldn't be happening. Like Martin Luther King said, "*you cannot defeat hatred with hatred, you must defeat it with love.*" A year without war would be a major victory for the world.

Terry Castleman, 9

Peace should be between everyone. If people are being mean, they are just trying to work out their anger. We should try to bring peace instead of anger into the world.

Amanda Slaughter, 10

Peace is when there is no violence and everybody is nice, even at school.

Sneha Krishnau, 9

Peace makes everything better. Try to make things better for people who will come after you.

Ciro Podany, 12

74

Peace is when
the whole country
comes together.
We wouldn't have racism
We'd all be one people.

Lucinda Watson, 12

Peace should be a part of our lives.
Everyone has some peacefulness in them,
but I guess that some people need to find it.
We have to make sure
we show the peace we have inside.

Elsinore Smidth, 13

75

Peace is happiness—everyone working together, teamwork. I think that war as a way to solve problems is really pathetic. You can't solve a problem by creating more problems. You have to find a way that is peaceful.

Lilah Clevey, 11

War makes me mad.
They shoot guns
and people get run over.
We should do peace-rallying.

Cole McCann-Phillips, 3

Peace is the medicine. What if war weren't an option.

Albert Brown, 8

Peace means that you have to not
  argue and that you should be nice to
  each other and be friends with each
  other; actually you don't have to be
  friends, but just…don't argue.
  Respect one another.
  No weapons. No fighting. No war.

Danielle Schatzman, 8

Instead of making war, I would have
  a championship tennis game between
  people who disagree. War kills and
  I hate the idea of killing.

Michelle Leason, 10

Peace is when everyone cares for
  each other and there are never any
  wars and you are allowed to go
  anywhere. No one is telling you that
  you can't go certain places.

Zeena Ojjeh, 9

peace

There is rarely
any peace for me in my
house living with
my 2-year-old brother Gabriel.

Eli Newbrun-Mintz, 7

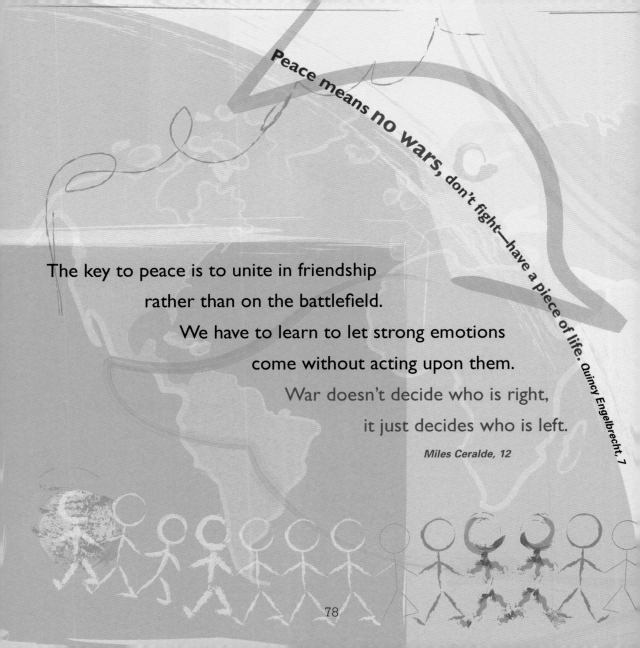

Peace means no wars, don't fight—have a piece of life. *Quincy Engelbrecht, 7*

The key to peace is to unite in friendship
rather than on the battlefield.
We have to learn to let strong emotions
come without acting upon them.
War doesn't decide who is right,
it just decides who is left.

Miles Ceralde, 12

Peace is just like

some invention that

makes everything work right.

Cortnay Cymrot, 10

If the world could be one way,

I would choose the nicest way.

If the world could be one way,

I would choose the happiest way.

If the world could be one way,

I would choose the funniest way.

If the world could be one way,

I would choose the peaceful way.

If the world could be one way,

I would choose the loving way.

If the world could be one way.

Lauren Moscarello, 8

Healing for a better world

I get really sad when animals die.
I wish the dolphins could stay forever.
Animals love each other and they give kisses.
We should give blessings to animals
to be healthy and happy.

Isabel Rauchle, 3

HEA

You can't always
take;
you have to **give**.

Sophia Gilchrist, 11

Learn to respect others and be non-harming, and don't argue about religions. It is important to always be loving and kind to others.

Alex Rauchle, 7

Be yourself. Don't try
to be someone else.

Mable Herrick, 7

LING

We should treat animals like

they're another person, a person

that you love.

Jill Meserve, 11

I have three animals: a leopard, a cheetah and a dog. I feed them and give them water.

Alexander Palmer, 5

Some animals are dying and we want to take care of them. Take care of animals, feed them, make them have baths. I hope all the dolphins will stay alive for a long time. We should ask the earth if it's okay to put our houses where we want them to go, because it might be a place where we hurt the earth or a plant. Take care of the earth.

Anya Rauchle, 6

My favorite animal is the red wolf. They are an endangered species and I would like to respect them a little bit more. Don't hunt them and don't kill the surroundings around them so they don't die as much.

Kaylie Kathleen Williams, 10

I love horses and cats and dogs and hamsters and guinea pigs. I like baby pigs. I like all animals. We should make boats with extra metal, so they won't leak oil and kill fish and birds.

Michelle Leason, 10

If you don't take care of Mother Earth, she could punish you with her animals. Keep her animals safe, keep the earth beautiful, don't cut down too many trees, and use natural stuff—don't use stuff that makes the world icky with pollution. I think that since **God was your creator you should take care of his place.**

Cali Slepin, 8

My favorite animals are African animals: cheetahs and lions and leopards. I'm going to go to Africa when I'm either 22 or 21 and tell them to stop poaching those animals so people can go to the camps down there to look at the animals.

Marcus Christianson, 6

My favorite animals are the elephants. We shouldn't capture them. We should leave them free.

Caleb Mahoney, 6

To show animals you love them, you could give them food. You could find a nest of a bird and give them food so when the birds flew back they could eat it.

Katherine Mary Scotnicki, 5

We should care for animals. The only time you should ever dissect an animal is if it has a disease, so you can learn from it.

Alex Leason, 12

I think we should
be respectful to other
people around the
world, not just people of
your same religion or
nation. I think we can be nice
to everyone from a different
country who comes into our
country. We need to give
them support.

Elliott Stone, 12

People might look mean on
the outside, but they have a good heart.
We should look for the goodness in
people's hearts. I had the idea to pick flowers from my
mom's garden and sell them at the market, and then
give the money to poor people, so they could have a place to live
and something to eat.

Mallory Bragg, 8

I want to unite the world. I just don't understand racism and
things like that. We are all the same and we all are one. We
are different in tiny little ways and somehow that makes
some people hate other people who seem different. Try and love
someone who you don't.

Sarah Wiener, 13

Just because someone is different doesn't mean they're bad. Just because a lot of people think they know something, it doesn't mean it is. Animals teach us lessons. They are smarter than us. You don't see a whole lot of animals fighting over one thing; we can learn from them.

Nadia Herman, 10

on't be mean to people who don't look like you.

Caleb Mahoney, 6

Dare to be different. My dad said that to me once in a speech competition, *"Dare to be different."* I think that's a lot like life, because in life you have no idea what's going to happen. You cannot be afraid to go out and do something. If you sit back and are afraid—*"Oh, should I do this?"*—you'll never get anywhere in life.

Eric Brandon, 13

I think it's really important that people live their lives calmly and not harm or hurt someone else. To live calmly is to be centered and focused and present where you are and not dwelling on a certain emotion that could harm others. Meditation helps you stay present, not daydreaming, noticing what's going on around you. It helps because it opens up your heart to other people.

Miles Ceralde, 12

87

We should behave respectfully towards nature; tend
the Earth with kindness, because it gives us so much.
I had a pet mouse. It's the only animal I ever had.
Instead of getting a rambunctious dog, I got this small
gray mouse. I had to be so gentle and careful with it.
Animals can teach us in this way—how to be more
tender and gentle.

Zoe Loughran Brezsny, 12

We should cut down less forests, because I really
like animals and the loss of habitats can cause
extinction of animals. Also, trees provide oxygen,
and we breathe in oxygen. So, cut down less forests.

Rachel Knodel, 11

Mother Earth is basically the trees: if you chop them
down, then that's like chopping one of her arms
off. Mother Earth would have lots of arms if all the
trees were her arms. If you cut down the trees
it's like cutting your arms off. You shouldn't chop
them off, because it hurts. Don't litter or spit on the
ground. I try to tell my friends not to do that.
Littering is bad for the Earth; animals could come
around and say, *"Yum food."* But litter is bad
for them—once they eat it, they choke and die.

Connor Barnett, 8

Earth is like a person, if you don't treat it with respect it won't be your friend.

Sophie Gilchrist, 11

I know that Mother Earth goes to sleep in winter and wakes up in spring. We should not cut down a lot of the forest and only use a little of the lumber; only take as much as you need. And the same with the plants: only take as much as you need especially if the animals eat those plants—like cabbage and carrots. We should respect the animals.

Tyler Briant Nierstedt, 6

The world would be a better place if people stopped using so much paper.

Eli Newbrun-Mintz, 7

We should recycle more and re-use things more than we do now.

Danny Sacks, 11

We should think of things as they really are—like rocks—people just look at them and say, "Oh, just another rock." But if you think about it, rocks are a lot. We should not take anything for granted. We should treat animals a lot differently than we do now. We should not kill animals inhumanely. I wouldn't want to be slaughtered inhumanely. I would like to be fed right, to have a nice habitat or environment. I wouldn't like to be caged up like in some zoos. I wouldn't like to be in a circus tamed by lion tamers. I think that's extremely cruel—big magnificent beasts being trained to jump through a hoop. It's just not right.

Eric Brandon, 13

Grown-ups are sometimes a little bit stuck up
about their beliefs and I think they should give kids
more responsibility. Just because we're younger
doesn't mean we don't know stuff. There's definitely
stuff that kids see that grown-ups are blind to.
So, I think adults should listen to kids.

Siena Hood, 12

When adults tell kids not to do something, they
shouldn't do those things themselves.

Alex Rauchle, 7

Sometimes adults are too small. I think parents should
set a positive example for children.

Julia Egger, 13

Be more patient and caring with kids.

Michelle Leason, 10

I think what adults should do is any child who
doesn't have a home or a family, they should try to
find somebody to take care of them or a home
for them to stay in.

Lila Hood, 8

Sometimes adults really misunderstand kids;
they think, *"Oh, they're kids and they don't know
anything."* Adults should listen more to children,
it would make it easier for us to be kids.

Lucinda Watson, 12

Maybe adults should actually listen to
our ideas instead of disregarding them.
I think some governments should
listen to its people more, considering a
government is its people.

Stewart Gruen, 11

Don't be too hard on children when they get into trouble.

Jill Meserve, 11

Don't hurt your kids, and be happy.

Kylle Koenig, 12

When grown-ups say things, it mostly goes
because kids don't exactly have that much power.
When you grow up and become an adult
you sort of lose your kid, and you turn into your
parents, or someone who's more of the boss
over the kids. It would be cool if when we grew up,
we remembered everything about being a kid
and made it easier to be a kid.

Cole Page, 12

I think we kids should have a little more freedom and we should be listened to a little more and be respected and be treated more equally. Maybe parents should have a little more rights, but it shouldn't be like they are Kings and Queens and we are just their servants.

Karl Bach, 11

If I were King or Queen of the...

...first have everybody find their inner peace and kindness and inner strength, so that they could help people around them. It would be important to make sure that everybody in the world knows how their food is grown, to be aware of the pesticides on our food, and to grow our own food, like in community gardens. We should take better care of our planet. If we use all of our resources and aren't careful, there won't be a good planet for future generations. I just hope that one day everybody in the world will be happy and peaceful and loving. We can all start with ourselves: be as kind and caring as you can be.

Elsinore Smidth, 13

...make people feel better, help them to find work. It's like the story about the fish, give a person a fish and you feed them, give them a fishing pole and they can feed themselves many times. I would end segregation in schools. There are too many groups. If you are on the outside group, you can be happy by having imaginary friends. I have an imaginary friend who is a tree.

Alisa Billig, 9

...cure all diseases, like AIDS and cancer. I'd also colonize other planets so that we could house people somewhere when it got too crowded here. I'd like us to have a happier world. Live happy.

Adrian Franco, 11

...world with unlimited powers, I would...

...help everyone in the world because the world is our home.

Anya Rauchle, 6

...tell everyone to be nice
and don't be mean
to each other. Don't
fight and don't have
wars, play Barbies
and ponies with
each other instead.

Madison Naomi Schobinger, 6

...shoot people with a tranquilizer gun that
would turn them into nice people. If you were nice
to people, they would probably be nice to you.

Mattias Hanson, 10

...plant more flowers and trees and make more parks
around the world. I would like the world to be
more peaceful.

Evan Cranston, 9

If I were Queen or King of the

...take all weapons away and make all the bad guys
lighten up and do something to not be bad anymore.
I would recommend that we not make bad movies,
like killing movies. I would put everybody in homes
and not let anybody be homeless. I would have
something to prevent people from drinking heavily
and driving. I'd take all cigarettes away. I would help
the animals that are on the street, and if they have
any wounds I'd take them to the veterinarian.

Danielle Schatzman, 8

...clean houses for people who are disabled, and
help them get everything organized. I'd help them to
get outdoors, out into the world. I'd also help
people make better choices on how to live. God
gave us something really special, he gave us the
ability to make our own choices.

Justin Jones, 11

...make peace in the world. I wouldn't let people
fight. I would make them sit down and settle it out. I
would give water from the clouds. It would make
rainwater to help the trees to live because if they
die then there's no oxygen. I might give this book to
my best friend Sam and his mother, Betsy, because
I've known them for six years of my life, and I'm
only 7 years old.

Quincy Engelbrecht, 7

...shut off all power
plants and have everyone
use solar energy. If we don't
start doing that now, global warming is
going to heat up the planet and make everything die. If we keep destroying
things, the Earth will fall apart. I don't want to wake up one morning and find
everything dead.

Lilah Clevey, 11

world with unlimited powers, I would...

...be sure that everyone had enough to eat and a place to sleep and that every child had parents that took care of them and had parents like mine who love them and love to be with them all the time. No one would steal or hurt anyone else. We would all share what we had and all enjoy everything.

Lauren Moscarello, 8

If I were King or Queen of th

...make sure everyone had electric cars so we would not have to care about gas, and we would not have as many wars as we do now, and we would not hurt our environment. I would also make sure people used solar energy and no one would be allowed to go poaching or hunting.

Lauren Steinbaum, 12

...make the world safe. I would try to stop wars all over the world and I would disarm all chemical and nuclear weapons. Most people fight about something they want or that they think is theirs or for something that was taken from them. Basically, just try not to take something by force.

Alon Sacks, 9

...not spend a lot of money on weaponry but spend it on people. Help people who need help. Your life is not as long as you think, so you should do as much good as possible.

Josh Herman, 10

... have a meeting with a bunch of people from all over the world, and I'd tell them to compromise. I'd say, *"Okay, we just don't go to war, we just try to settle things in a different way. We don't need war, it's just killing more people."* We could try to agree with each other and listen to each other, to other people's recommendations. Even if you don't agree, don't cut them off, just listen. Then when it's your turn, you can tell them.

Carrie Brandon, 9

...bring people from different countries to another country so they could see how people live and maybe that can spread around the world. That might help peace, because people can get a sense of how other people live, in other cultures.

Alexandra Goldstein, 10

world with unlimited powers, I would...

...ask for everyone to be caring of others, to the environment, to animals and plants. Caring is acting with compassion towards other beings.

Miles Ceralde, 12

...stop killing wild endangered animals and investing in tobacco. I think we should start investing more in education and schools and the homeless, instead of tobacco and stuff we don't even need.

TJ Dempsey, 11

...tell people to not make a mess in our world.

Gayle Henry, 12

If I were **Queen** or **King** of th

...make it be so there would be no cars. Instead, there would be electric fields that would pull you along. Everyone would ride bikes and you'd go down the hill but there'd be some electric field that would pull you up again. So you wouldn't have to ride up the hill. You'd just ride everywhere and there'd be electric planes and solar stuff. I think we should find a really good president. A good president wouldn't want to go to war.

Luke Garrison, 13

...end the world's hunger. I would have supermarkets where the stuff that maybe is really expensive in other stores could be really cheap for people who don't have as much money so they could afford a lot more food.

Lauren Christianson, 10

...make community centers for people who are sad so they could become more involved in life and make more schools for kids.

Chelsea Cymrot, 12

...give money to the Third World countries.

Angelique Traub, 12

world with unlimited powers, I would...

...bring world peace.

Kylee Larsen, 12

...take the leaders from all the countries
who want peace and have them be the king and
queen together, a united front, and have them
make all decisions together. They would be peaceful
and loving.

Siena Hood, 12

...make the world be pretty instead of ugly and
everybody happy, and when they were sad I would
have them come and discuss it.

Zoe Goldberg, 6

If I were King or Queen of th

...explore outer space because that is our future.
I would get out into space and make colonies
and better space ships so that when this world
comes to an end we have another world to go to.
It will happen at some point. I would also help
teach people who have a disability or who have
given up in life. I would show them a bunch of
famous people who have their disability and how
they make it in the world. I would help people that
have given up on life and don't want to go any
farther, even the elderly.

Coray Runge, 13

...tell everyone that you'd have to be nice at least
for a day, so that they could see how to get along.
Elena Scott, 12

...be a respectful queen. I would respect everyone
else and respect the Earth that we live on now.
Kaylie Kathleen Williams, 10

...let God choose what I should do. I think that
God would want us to make love and make peace
and let everyone be free. I had a dream where
God was hurt from sadness, because on Earth there
were lots of people who were sad. There were
angels there, I couldn't see them, they were just all
this light. The angels came to help God with the
sadness, and when the sadness in God was healed,
then all the people of the Earth were healed too.
Amanda Slaughter, 10

...ask my soldiers to
make a bunch of
new houses for the
homeless.

Michelle Leason, 10

orld with unlimited powers, I would...

We need to read more books and drink more tea. It's important to slow down and relax. In today's society, people are very uptight and rush around. To have time to sit and read and drink tea is a calming way to just sink into life. Laughter is the best thing. I laugh a lot. People should laugh more. Don't take things so seriously. And question authority—it helps you to be strong, and it helps you to know what's going on.

Zoe Loughran Brezsny, 12

Use only as much money as you need. Millionaires have a lot of money, they should only use stuff that they need instead of buying humongous mansions and stuff like that.

Tyler Briant Nierstedt, 6

Always leave a moment for yourself; never be in too much of a rush.

Lilah Clevey, 11

The world would be a better place with no drugs.

Tifton Medicinehorse, 11

We should give money to poor people and clean all the dirty places. There should be no strict rules.

Sneha Krishnau, 9

I think every country has rights and deserves a healthy environment and a good supply of money so everyone has what they need.

Steven Chen, 9

Generosity is important, which is giving money to people who don't have money. You don't need money to live a good life, but you do need a home.

Anji Herman, 10

We should go to old folks homes and sing. I used to do that for my grandpa and it made everybody there feel really good. Everybody would gather around and my Uncle Bobby would play piano and sing and it really cheered them up and that felt good. It goes back to love. If you love somebody, they'll love you back.

Carrie Brandon, 9

Never give up.
If you give up,
you never realize
your goals
in life.

Chelsea Cymrot, 12

If you
work hard and
are determined to
make your life
better,
it will get better.

Lauren Steinbaum, 12

not good now, there is always the hope to get a better life. Believe that it will turn out okay, even if it's not good now. There are other people in the world who believe for you, who want to help. Have hope and love everyone you know. If you don't like someone, try to respect their position. Maybe you'll learn that you really like them. That's how the whole world unites.

Elena Scott, 12

The Indians used to say there is a wheel in your stomach and it has **sharp ends**, and when you lie it turns and **pokes** you and makes you **feel bad**. If you **keep lying,** finally the ends will **wear off** and you can't **feel** it anymore—**you can't even feel the bad things you do to other people** because you've lied so much.

Emma Rubinowitz, 11

Respect everything.

Respect the Earth.

Be helpful for one another.

Be courteous, kind, truthful.

Don't be harming animals.

Don't kill anybody else.

Treat people good and they'll treat you good.

Thomas Medicinehorse, 12

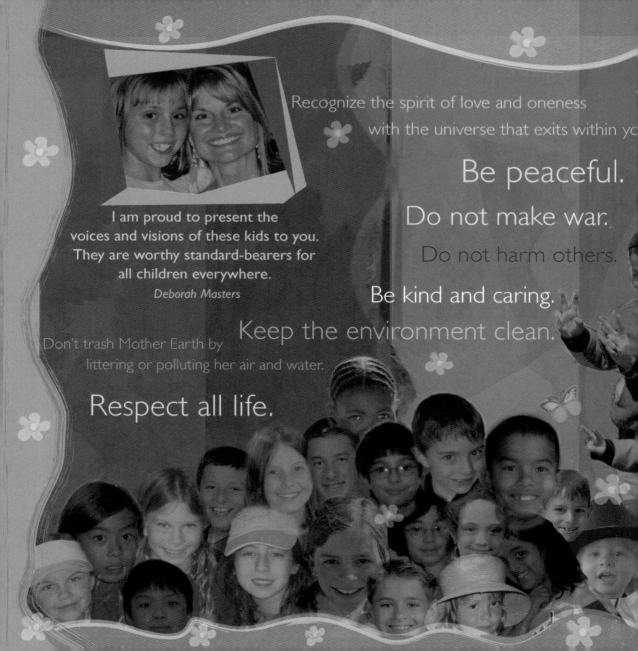

Recognize the spirit of love and oneness
with the universe that exits within yo

I am proud to present the
voices and visions of these kids to you.
They are worthy standard-bearers for
all children everywhere.

Deborah Masters

Be peaceful.

Do not make war.

Do not harm others.

Be kind and caring.

Keep the environment clean.

Don't trash Mother Earth by
littering or polluting her air and water.

Respect all life.

Treat animals well and **don't destroy** their habitats.

Preserve forests. Distribute wealth.

Care for children.

Feed the poor. Help the homeless.

Provide education, housing,
and healthcare for everyone.

Do community service.

Laugh a lot.